CANAL WALKS

JULIA
BRADBURY

A huge thanks again to the team for their support and creative spirit. In particular, thanks to Eric Harwood for your friendship and editorial guidance, Clare Jones for your creatively rich suggestions and sense of humour, Gina my sister for keeping the momentum going and being No.1 Platter Queen. The programmes are not possible without the whole crew – thank you all for making the pictures (and sounds) come to life. My gratitude to Richard Klein and Clare Paterson at the BBC – they would be walks to nowhere without you. Finally Mum and Dad, Chrissi and Michael – thank you.

Frances Lincoln Ltd
4 Torriano Mews
Torriano Avenue
London NW5 2RZ
www.franceslincoln.com

British Library Cataloguing in Publication Data
A catalogue record for this book is available from the British Library.

ISBN: 978-0-7112-3249-5

Printed and bound in Slovenia

9 8 7 6 5 4 3 2 1

RIGHT: Painted canal jug on the Kennet & Avon Canal.
PREVIOUS PAGES: Higher Wharf, Bradford-on-Avon.

CONTENTS

Introduction	8
Llangollen	14
Worcester & Birmingham	38
Caledonian	60
Kennet & Avon	84
Index	110

Moored fishing boat on the Caledonian Canal.

The last time I sat down to write the preamble for a book, I could revel in the function of the machine that inspired that series of walks – railways. I was sitting on a train while writing – the *clunk clunk* rhythm of the journey coaxing my words along. Although Dr Beeching's cruel slashes through the railway network back in the 1960s left huge chasms of lost industry and connectivity, some trains *did and* still *do* run across the country; railway lines still carry people and cargo from A to Z. By the 1960s the same could not be said of the UK's canal network. Its demise was almost total, which seems incredible considering what a big noise canals were.

Canals were at the forefront of the Industrial Revolution in this country. Roads were just emerging from muddy beginnings and the only way to transport any quantity of products around was by packhorse. In the mid eighteenth century the 3rd Duke of Bridgewater needed a reliable way to transport his coal to Manchester. He commissioned the engineer James Brindley to build the Bridgewater Canal, the first major British canal to open in 1761. Regarded as an engineering wonder it attracted great attention and spawned the beginning of a vast network. The new canals were a smash hit, and there were still jobs for the horses. Horse-drawn canal boats could carry thirty tonnes each, with only one horse doing the work. The canal system soon connected the country, becoming the cause and effect of rapid industrialisation. The period between the 1770s and the 1830s is often referred to as the 'Golden Age' of British canals. And, as with every big business with vast sums of money at stake, things got dirty. 'Canal mania' spread, investment funds were created where people could buy shares in a newly-floated company and immediately sell them on for a profit, regardless of whether the canal was ever in the black, or even built. Investors profited from dividends, businesses profited from the cheaper transport of raw materials and goods. There was rivalry as well. At one point the Worcester & Birmingham Canal and the

Julia arrives at Loch Lochy, the end goal for her Caledonian Canal Walk.

Birmingham Canal Navigations Main Line Canal ran only seven feet apart, but commercial hostilities made sure that they were never connected. At its height more than two thousand miles of canals thrived and bobbed along.

Early in the twentieth century things started to go wrong for canals. There were brief surges during the first and second world wars but basically the waterways were abandoned in favour of road and rail transport, and by the 1950s coal was about the only thing being delivered via canals to waterside factories which had no other convenient access. And then the Clean Air Act of 1956 put paid to that – factories were forced to consider other fuels or close completely. 1962 saw a startlingly harsh winter and boats were frozen to their moorings for weeks on end. The British Railways Board (now British Waterways) formally ceased commercial carrying that same year. One of the last carrying contracts was to a jam factory near London in 1971 – a sticky end.

Today, millions relish the UK's canals for very different reasons. Canal holidays are popular; people live on canals, cycle alongside canals and walk alongside canals. The Industrial Revolution is far behind us and poncy leisure/lifestyle pursuits are where it's at. I of course love the poncy leisure aspect. That's what I do. And it was a real pleasure poncing about on these four walks last Autumn. As ever our filming schedule was tight, time in short supply, and that meant waiting for good weather was not an option. We started the Worcester and Birmingham Canal walk late one afternoon and it was sheeting it down. We delayed and delayed, hoping that the wet would give way just a little. T'was not to be and I opened the programme in head to toe waterproofs. Unless your name begins with 'Red Riding' it is hard to look good in a hood. It's not that I mind the rain and we are all used to the outdoor purists' expression 'there's no such thing as the wrong weather, just the wrong clothes' but when you're filming I can assure you there *is* such a thing as the wrong weather. Camera and sound equipment are not at maximum efficacy in the wet. We battled on and I met our first contributor Graham Fisher, a pony-tailed canal enthusiast, on the footbridge just outside the Mailbox in the heart of Brum and near my start point in Gas Street Basin. He said 'Julia may I just say you're the same in person as you are on the telly. Just lovely'. Actually Graham, you can, thank you! If anything can raise the spirits in situations like that, it's good old fashioned flattery. I bounded off with a spring in my soggy boot, ready for the next section. Then the camera stopped. Deep joy. Day 0.5 of the Worcester & Birmingham canal walk could have started better . . .

The first time I visited the Kennet and Avon Canal was in mid winter. It was frozen over and the towpaths were covered in a thick blanket of white fluffy snow. The country had come to a stand-still – 'surprise snow' catching the nation out once again. And it wasn't just the roads that got clogged up. Try moving a narrowboat through a thick crust of ice. When it was built in 1810, the Kennet and Avon Canal was the Industrial Revolution equivalent of the M4, but with a speed limit of 4mph, not 70. That day the boats were moving at ground speed zero. Residents and visitors used to moving where they want when they want on the 87-mile waterway were resigned to their last docking position, frozen in place. It was a beautiful shimmering icy scene. During winter when you peep through the little windows everyone always looks so cosy inside, stoves aglow, streaks of hot smoke puffing out into the cold winter air. It was quite different in the spring. The K and A is a buzzy canal and you can feel the living rhythm of it pulse along its banks. There is a real community feel to this waterway; people hop on and off one another's boats and cycle up and down the banks with open trailers of groceries bouncing behind them. Fleur, a clothes designer, and Johnny, her boat-building husband, live on the canal with their two children Theo and Laurie. Four of them living an adventure on a narrow compact boat called 'Gyptian'. Amazingly the children have never fallen in to the water and seem like utterly happy little people. I can't imagine sharing such a tiny space on a boat but I'm slightly covetous of their emancipated lifestyle. Further along, the charming Sydney Gardens offers an unusual expanse of open space on a canal walk; this is Bath's oldest park, straight out of a Jane Austen novel. No really. Sydney Gardens was a 'resort of leisure' for nineteenth century gentry and Jane came here to hang out when she lived in Bath. When one attended gala events in the gardens back then the treats included 'cold ham and tongue, spirits, bottled porter, cider, perry, all as reasonable as possible, the prices of which will be affixed on the bills of fare and placed in every conspicuous part of the Garden'. I just had a cup of tea from a paper cup and a muesli bar.

The Llangollen Canal was a complete surprise and delight to me. The navigable but unpronounceable Pontcysyllte Aqueduct is an absolute treat. Who would expect a roller-coaster style ride on a canal? It may not be a super-speedy crossing but I couldn't believe my eyes when Peter Jones asked me to climb aboard and I peered over the side looking 126 feet down onto the River Dee. In these days of health and safety gone crackers you simply wouldn't be allowed to construct the same thing again – I didn't even wear a high vis vest – ha! (They're essential for so many activities these days you'd be amazed). I didn't expect showbiz stories on this walk, but the annual musical Eisteddfod is held in a pavilion that you can see quite clearly from the banks of the canal and this is where Pavarotti won an early prize singing with an Italian choir – a prize that inspired his operatic career. He returned to Llangollen more than forty years later to give a thank you concert and rumour has it that the hotel he stayed in had to knock down a wall in the bedroom to accommodate his mass. He also ate not one, not two but three tiramisus after one light supper. I bet he needed a good walk after that! I met a lovely group of lady walkers along the banks of the Llangollen who had christened themselves 'The Stridettes' after their respective husbands' walking group 'The Striders'. One lady told me I was a bit of an inspiration and whenever she was feeling jaded on a walk she'd say to herself 'come on, think of Julia – stride out Christine, stride out!' We had a little laugh and then I posed for some phone pics so they could prove to the other halves that we'd actually met. I can't wait to use that phrase on camera now. Come on Julia – stride out, STRIDE OUT!

The Caledonian Canal is a real treat because you get to walk an easy route against a backdrop of stunning rugged scenery. We started our walk at the Corpach Sea Lock, which means one of our first views was Ben Nevis. And if you're only expecting quaint little narrow boats, think again – Thomas Telford wanted to connect two sides of the country via

Julia stands 126 feet high on the Llangollen Canal's Pontcysllte Aqueduct.

this waterway, and the channels were to be big enough for ships. Which is the first thing I saw when we began filming in Scotland; a bloody great ship, full of smiling tourists all waving out of the portholes and off the decks mouthing 'what are you filming?'. Neptune's Staircase lock is the longest in the UK (made up of eight locks that lift the boats nearly 20 metres) and it is a pretty good thigh burner to get things pulsing, but that's as tough as it gets on this walk. I can picture the buzz and bustle of the 900 or so navvies who dug the channel by hand, fuelled by whisky, more than two hundred years ago. Ivor McKay looks as if he's been operating the Moy Bridge (the only manually controlled bridge left on the canal) all his life. We had a lovely natter about his years on 'The Cal' and then we took the opportunity to have a crew brew. Ivor had biscuits, we had chocolate bars – it was the perfect trade. A couple of photos later and we pushed on for the final stretch, to the incredible view of Loch Lochy. As we arrived, some gentle rain started to fall and then a rainbow appeared over the water. The props department in the sky had come up with the goods once again. Who says television isn't magic?

stream through the skies

Surrounded by a limestone escarpment of mountains and divided by the turbulent waters of the River Dee, the valley of Llangollen posed considerable obstacles to Principal Engineer Thomas Telford. His bold response was the making of his reputation. The soaring Pontcysllte Aqueduct recently earned the prestigious title of a World Heritage site. It's an icon of engineering that takes water and allows it to fly.

This walk will allow you to delve into the history and the engineering behind Telford's masterpiece and explore the quiet valley which he so cleverly navigated. And for those with a head for heights, the end of this walk is a highlight in every sense as you'll be able to cross the magnificent 'Stream through the Skies'.

Walkers with a head for heights cross the vertigo inducing Pontcysllte Aqueduct on the Llangollen Canal.

history of the canal

The 6 mile long Llangollen Canal was planned as early as 1791 as a branchline of the proposed eastern mainline canal in Shropshire that was to link the Rivers Mersey and Dee with the River Severn. This grand plan, that would have linked a canal route through Wales, never came to fruition. Financial backers dried up, but the Llangollen section survived, serving a key purpose as a feeder to the main Ellesmere Canal, drawing water off the River Dee at Horseshoe Falls. Work began in 1804 and was completed in 1808 with Thomas Telford as part-time Principal Engineer or Agent and Thomas Denson as Resident Engineer. Once the feeder canal was built however, it provided another benefit, providing a key transport artery to the slate quarries and the limestone works.

LEFT: High above the River Dee. ABOVE: Narrowboats get a bird's eye view when they cross the Pontcysllte Aqueduct.

In 1846 it became part of the Shropshire Union Railways Company but the following year was taken over by the London and Northwestern Railway (LNWR). With the arrival of the railways, commercial transport on the canal was dramatically reduced by the late nineteenth century and had all but completely ceased by World War II.

The canal was kept open however, because of its importance as a supplier of water to the Shropshire Union Canal, the steam engines at Chester Station and some houses in the Crewe area. Over six million gallons a day are now metered into the canal at Horseshoe Falls.

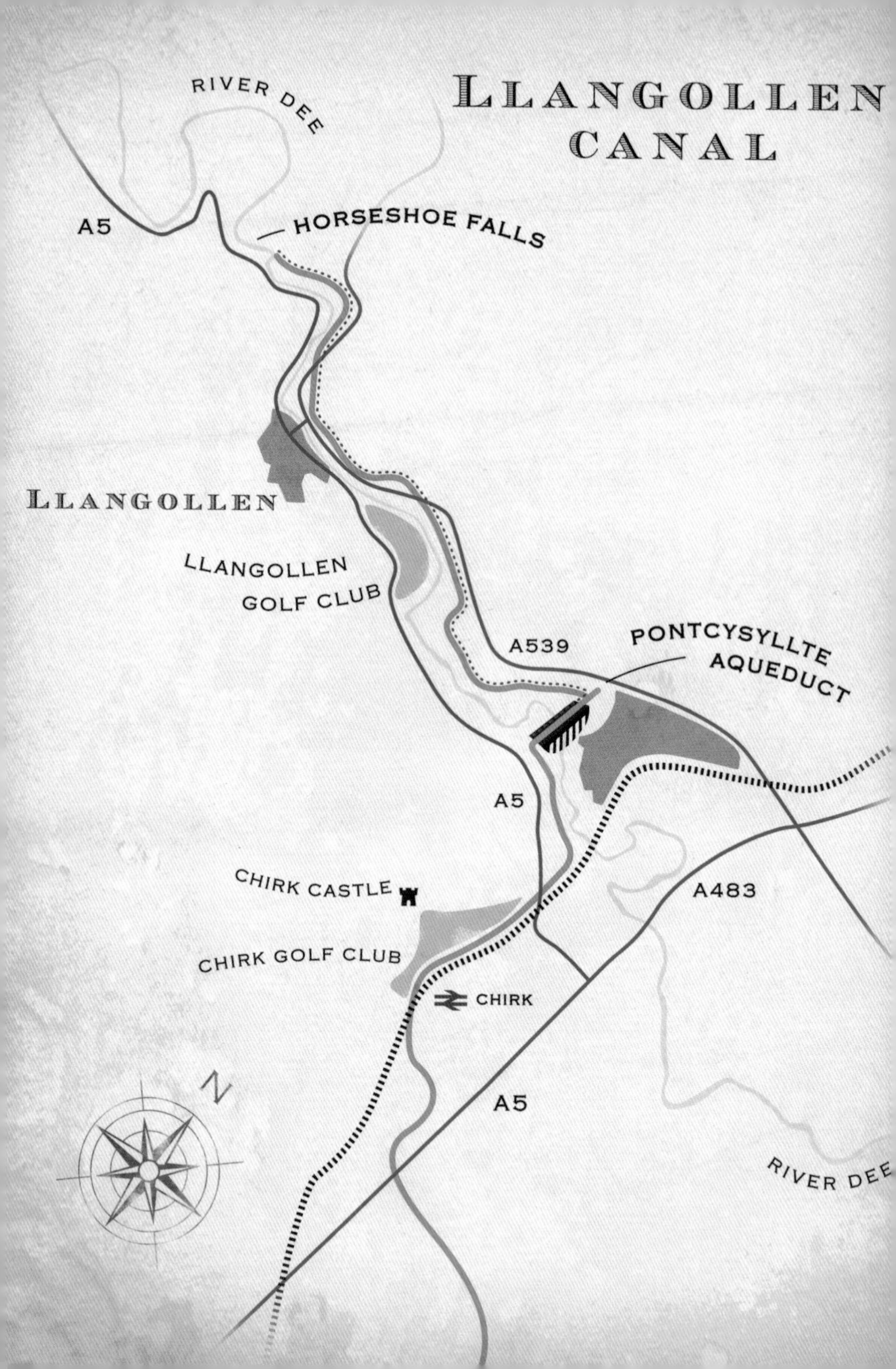

LLANGOLLEN CANAL

RIVER DEE

A5

HORSESHOE FALLS

LLANGOLLEN

LLANGOLLEN
GOLF CLUB

A539

PONTCYSYLLTE
AQUEDUCT

A5

CHIRK CASTLE

A483

CHIRK GOLF CLUB

CHIRK

A5

RIVER DEE

N

THE WALK

Horseshoe Falls to the Pontcysllte Aqueduct

6 miles / 9.6 kilometres

OVERVIEW

By the late eighteenth century the map of Britain had changed forever. A new and growing network of transport superhighways dominated the landscape. Canals had arrived connecting towns and cities with Britain's industrial heartlands and export hubs. In this flourishing climate Thomas Telford, a rising star in the field of civil engineering was appointed to link a remote and rural Wales with England and beyond. My walk follows a section of this growing canal network that was actually an offshoot, a kind of branchline. This section wasn't even originally built for boats. It was a feeder canal, designed simply to supply water to the rest of the western network. Today, the 6 mile stretch from Horseshoe Falls to the Pontcysllte Aqueduct provides an idyllic towpath walk.

STAGE 1

Horseshoe Falls to Pentre Felin

Castell Dinas Bran clings to the hillside above Llangollen.

If you have the time for a slight diversion it's well worth making the effort to make the shortish climb up to Castell Dinas Bran, the dramatic ruins of a medieval castle, which perch above the town of Llangollen. I promise you there's really not so much huff and puff involved for the rewarding views it offers. From up here the walk is laid out in front of you, a bird's eye view of the valley, which the canal so cleverly navigated. Not only do you get a stunning view of the rolling foothills, the wooded slopes of the Vale of Llangollen, and the jagged limestone escarpment edge, but you can also begin to see how these natural obstacles stood in the way of the canal engineers.

At the time of its construction the canal network was expanding rapidly, spreading from northern England across the Cheshire Plains and into this northeastern corner of Wales. But when it got here, not only did the engineers need to carve a path through this valley but they also had to get across the turbulent waters of the River Dee some 126 feet below. Bridging this gap posed a major engineering conundrum. The phenomenal Pontcysllte Aqueduct was the spectacular answer.

The real start point of this walk is actually on the banks of the River Dee and intriguingly it ends way above it, 126 feet higher, cleverly crossing the river that feeds the whole canal system. This is not just a walk along a towpath. This is a walk which steps back into a world of industrial heritage and reveals some of the incredible engineering that was needed to make this route even possible. Once the Llangollen Canal was built it wasn't simply an engineering triumph, it paved the way for a whole new world of industry and trade.

This was the first walk I did for my BBC television series so I was keen to get my bearings and learn a little bit more about this route which already seemed to be so full of surprises. So I arranged to meet a local expert. Bryn Hughes is a walking guide, tour leader and was born and bred in this valley. So

who better to shed a bit of light on the walk? We met at Horseshoe Falls, a local beauty spot with a key story to tell in this walk.

The first and most obvious thing which struck me about our rendezvous spot was that this arcing weir which cuts across the river, lovely as it is, was most definitely still not a canal. But as Bryn began to explain, this was Telford's ingenious method of drawing water from the River Dee into the canal system. One of the key problems for the canal engineers of this time was keeping their canals stocked with a constant supply of water. What Telford realised was that he had a plentiful supply of fresh water here and that if he was clever he could tap into this and use it to fill his canal network further afield.

By directing part of the river into a collecting reservoir, water could be channelled into the canal that's hidden just a short walk around the corner. Today the little pumphouse that sits between the river and the canal forces six million

LEFT: Horseshoe Falls on the River Dee.
ABOVE: Cruising the canal near Llangollen.

gallons of water into the network, which eventually makes it to homes in Crewe as drinking water.

On the other side of this building is the rather humble start of the canal. It definitely looks like a tight squeeze, which intriguingly doesn't appear to have ever been made with narrowboats in mind. But Bryn went on to explain that this section was never originally intended for boats, it was just designed as a feeder. There was no need to build a wide section to connect with the River Dee as goods and trade weren't transported by river, the waters were simply too turbulent. Great for whitewater kayakers today, not much good to trade back in the eighteenth century.

The other great thing about meeting a true local at the start of a walk is that you get the chance to clear up some matters of pronunciation early on. It's something of an occupational hazard for me, I'm always trying to learn tongue-twisting placenames that I need to wrap my mouth round and then try to remember. So on the banks of this humble branchline Bryn kindly gave me some lessons in the Welsh language. Not least of all because the prize at the end of my walk, Telford's masterpiece aqueduct, was a bit of a mouthful.

'Pontcysllte' can roughly be broken down phonetically into 'Pont' and then 'c-suth-te' and it seemed to sound better the quicker I tried to roll it out, although I have to admit I did sound a little bit like I had a pair of stuck dentures, unlike Bryn's lovely lilting accent. When translated, 'Pont' means 'bridge' and 'cysyllte' means 'to join' so – 'the bridge that joins', a very apt name indeed for my final goal.

It's all thanks to the canal that my walk today is one without a steep climb. The route which the canal took, had to be the easiest and most efficient. So thanks to a well laid out towpath this walk hugs the contours of the valley and stays at a nice steady level throughout.

As the first real stretch gets underway you'll find yourself walking through what feels like a lovely green corridor of overhanging trees and pockets of ferns that sway to your step. There's time indeed to soak up these very tranquil surroundings and the chance to enjoy an altogether relaxed pace. There's definitely something very peaceful about walking alongside water. Watching the leaves and the foliage drift along the surface while elegant fronds wave at you from the canal bank is mesmerising.

But life wasn't always quite so peaceful on this canal. This valley and the surrounding area was a rich seam of coal, slate, limestone, wood and wool. The canal provided a way to tap into these. It might have been built to supply water but once it arrived new opportunities for trade were quickly taken up.

After only a mile or so of the walk you'll arrive at Pentre Felin, which was once the site of a slateworks. Today the warehouse buildings, which once buzzed with life, are occupied by a motor museum. Sitting on the side of the supporting wall you can also see how that, at this point,

A clearly laid out towpath makes for some easy walking along the Llangollen Canal.

Telford and his engineers had already cleverly managed to get the canal 16 feet or so above the River Dee. It's a sign of things to come at the end of my walk, where I'll be well and truly looking down on the river.

Wales is said to have 'roofed the world' and this quiet spot was part of that golden industrial age. Once it opened in 1845 the slateworks buzzed with life. In its heyday 65 loaders were employed. Horses rattled via a tramroad from the quarry above and inside the building, now occupied with vintage cars, slate was shaped and planed and then heaved onto the waiting canal boats. But it would be easy not to realise that there was so much activity here once upon a time. As a walker you could easily pass on through without giving it a second glance.

STAGE 2

Pentre Felin to Llangollen

Captain Jones' Llangollen horse-drawn boats still depart from the town centre wharf.

But trade did take off on the canal and canal boats once plied this section of my walk, bound for their next port of call, the bustling town of Llangollen. The trade boats might be gone today but there's still one very familiar canalside scene that is unique to Llangollen, a tradition that has been pulling in visitors for well over a hundred years.

The faint sound of the clip-clop of hooves and the light murmur of contented chatter are the hallmarks of one of the town's oldest attractions – the Llangollen horse-drawn canalboats. As I made my way along the towpath I was lucky enough to bump into today's owner, Peter Furniss, out on one of his trips along the canal. It's been a commonplace sight since 1884 when a rather interesting gentleman by the name of Captain Jones started the whole thing off.

Tourism was still in its infancy in those days. Captain Jones however, was ahead of his time and spotted a gap in the market. The story goes that he was a ship's captain with the White Star Line but one day he fell off the bridge of his ship, allegedly whilst drunk. The White Star Line, perhaps thinking it wasn't particularly good for their image to have a drunken Captain, pensioned him off. With his pension he purchased two redundant ship's lifeboats from the docks at Liverpool, brought them to Llangollen and started the horse-drawn boats of Llangollen.

In many ways this was the start of a new vein of life for this area. Trade on the canal boosted the fortunes of this valley, which then helped to nurture a new kind of business for the town in the shape of tourism. Only a short walk further on there's another unmistakable canalside view, which has been attracting its fair share of visitors to Llangollen.

You might just see a flash of white through the trees before you see its curving roof. But it's certainly unmissable once you get to the outskirts of town. This rather unusual tent-like structure is the International Eisteddfod Pavilion, rather like the millennium dome, just a mini version of it.

'Eisteddfod' is a Welsh word, which literally means 'to be sitting together' and its origins lie in the twelfth century Welsh tradition of gathering to celebrate language, poetry and literature. The first International Eisteddfod was held in 1947, to promote a message of post war peace. Today, in the first week of July each year, over five thousand artists, from over fifty different countries, perform and compete to audiences of more than fifty thousand. That means that over the years a lot of people have sung their little lungs out in there.

Locals say the International Eisteddfod is where 'Wales Welcomes the World'. It's even been the unexpected launch pad for some highbrow careers. In 1955 Pavarotti came to compete with his father and their choir from Modena. They won the Male Voice Choir competition, which he said was the most important experience of his life and inspired him to turn professional. He returned forty years later to give a triumphant and tearful free concert. Amazing to think this all takes place right next to the canal and as Peter said, maybe its in part all thanks to the arrival of the canal that the fortunes of this valley were able to prosper. Now there's the power of water.

After just over two miles the towpath now skirts alongside the edge of town. You can soon see it's a spot that today's cruising boats make a beeline for, making this stretch of canal one of the busiest in the UK. The basin at Llangollen is a cheerful swathe of colour with a clutch of narrowboats moored up for the night.

Approaching the Llangollen Basin where boats moor up for the night.

The town itself is clearly buzzing, attracting tourists and plenty of walkers, who just like me, are treading the towpath. And down in the town, the A5 road runs alongside the tumbling waters of the Dee, the steam railway straddles its bank and the canal looks down on both, three ages of transport sitting side by side.

The arrival of the railway in the 1860s however, sounded the death knell on the canal and the last tradeboat ploughed its waters on the eve of World War I. So it really is tourism which is now the main trade of this valley. But the canal remains the rich vein running through this town, people travel on it by boat, they come to walk its towpath, they even come here to sing alongside it.

STAGE 3

Llangollen to the Pontcysllte Aqueduct

The magnificent Pontcysllte Aqueduct.

After passing the old wharf building that is now the base for the horse-drawn canalboats, Llangollen seems to quickly fade into the background. The walk soon returns to a quiet corridor of shady trees, the rooftops of Llangollen gradually hidden by the leaves. The steady hum of holiday boats chugging their way along the canal is the only real sound to punctuate the breezy calm. The canal really has its own rhythms and lifeblood. I found myself stopping to chat to fellow walkers, waving at cyclists wheeling their way along the towpath and idling alongside boats chatting to cheery folks on board, enthused by their waterway forays. This towpath has created a vibrant world of its own that you can't help but find yourself getting drawn into.

It's easy to look at the boats today and think that it looks simple enough to while away a bit of time on board a modern narrowboat. But full time employment on a trade boat was not quite so easy. By the late nineteenth century, commercial traffic had reached its peak and 'fly-boats' ran all the way through to Llangollen. These were the 'express couriers' of their day travelling around the clock. Today's boaters certainly ease along at an altogether different pace. And would you believe it, Harrison Ford and Calista Flockart have even come here to escape Hollywood on a narrowboat holiday.

The next section of the walk however, is a clear reminder of what the engineers had to overcome to carve this route. Less than a mile after leaving Llangollen you can really see how difficult it must have been to channel through the sharp rock face that is so clearly visible. This wasn't blasted with dynamite; instead it was painstakingly cut by hand, with only the basic tools of a pick, shovel and barrow.

And because this slender route was never originally intended for heavy traffic it's created some interesting navigational challenges for today's novice boater. Bridge number 43 is the next obstacle en route. This swing bridge, which links farmland either side might make life for the cows a bit easier but for boaters there are only inches either side to squeeze through. As a boat approached to take on this steering challenge it also provided me with the chance to immerse myself in another great canal tradition – the art of 'gongoozling', a lovely old canal word, which simply means stopping, staring, and watching a bit of canal life go by. Getting through this gap is certainly a tight squeeze, requiring a steady hand.

Standing on the side of the canal and watching life roll by, you really do realise there's something about the pace of all this that's very different to other walks. You really slow down, which for me is a pretty novel thing. There is a certain simplicity to the walking that I really enjoy.

Today, boats (and walkers) can steadily chug their way along a pretty uncomplicated route. By following the natural contours of this valley Telford cleverly avoided the need for any locks. As the River Dee flows steadily downwards the canal instead sticks above it, hugging the valley side. Just after bridge 42 you really get a sense of just how far you've now travelled. Here, the tree-lined banks open out to glorious wide views and looking down you can see that you are well above the river. And this can only mean one thing. Telford's 'Bridge through the Skies' isn't far away.

Before I started on the final stretch of my walk I found a convenient bench to soak up this lovely view and have a quick breather before the final push. It just also happened to be a prime spot for a bit of towpath foraging. I met local lady, Sarah Marshall, who certainly knew a good blackberry spot when she saw one and had biked along the towpath with her two kids from Llangollen. Her youngsters shared their excited plans about making crumble whilst their adventurous Mum happily shared a bit of local knowledge about the area and what a haven it was for the outdoor lover with biking, climbing as well as walking right on the doorstep. She also reminded me that the prize at the end of my walk offered its

Negotiating the narrow gap at bridge 43.

own bit of adrenaline. When I told her I'd heard it was a long way down she just cheerily replied that it was a big drop but a great view and offered me a blackberry for the road. So any vertiginous fears were temporarily put aside for a chomp on some freshly plucked blackberries. I don't know, the power of food!

My walk continued at this rather nice steady pace, boats pootled alongside, bikers wheeled by and there were more cheerful 'hellos' from fellow walkers. The next major view however comes at bridge 34. You can barely make it out amongst the trees but look carefully and you'll find it, the first view of Telford's masterstroke – the Pontcysllte Aqueduct.

It took two hundred men and ten years but it was eventually completed in 1805 at a cost of just over £47,000 – that's just under three million by today's standards. Given the scale of the construction it's extraordinary that building it almost went by without hitch. Only one man died in the

The colourful Trevor Basin, a busy hub for boats preparing to cross 'the big one'.

process, which a contemporary account describes rather starkly: 'He experienced no suffering as the tremendous height from which he fell caused instant dissolution'. Reading that description was certainly warning enough for me to keep my feet firmly on the towpath.

Today, the thrilling bit is going across the aqueduct. The final stretch of the walk winds towards the Trevor Basin, where the canal swings south and boats gather to prepare to make the big crossing. It was also the spot where I hoped to find an intriguing local character – 'Jones the Boats', someone I'd heard had a head for heights and might just be able to help me cross 'the big one'.

Now if there's someone who knows this aqueduct then it's Peter Jones. He's been over it hundreds of times now, running trips for visitors in his beloved 'Eirlys' (Welsh for snowdrop) a lovely brightly coloured narrowboat. So, who better to cadge a lift with for my first brush with the 'big one'? After hopping on board, Peter explained the rules of the road for going across the aqueduct, which is certainly only wide enough for one boat at a time and even then it looks pretty tight. Basically, it's a simple system, if you can see a gap and all is clear, you can go. If you can't, you wait.

I'm not sure anything quite prepares you for this. As you steadily chug your way across, the view is slightly masked but the trees suddenly part and you become instantly aware not only of the grand view spreading out before you but also of the plunging depths below. Unlike on the towpath side there isn't a guardrail. Instead, on the canal side, there is nothing but free-hanging space (apparently it was considered too expensive to add one at the time of construction). It's just you and a lot of empty airiness. And as Peter informed me there's nothing else quite like it in the country. Over two hundred years old it's the highest navigable aqueduct in the UK.

It stands on eighteen stone pillars that were made from local stone, brought down from the hills around and dressed on site. The blocks are held together with a mortar, strengthened with ox blood and lime. Apparently seventeen hundred oxen were used in the process; so, probably not the best place to have been an ox.

But perhaps Telford's greatest act of genius was solving the final engineering problem of how to get the water across his mighty aqueduct arches. His answer was in fact a simple cast iron trough construction. He'd previously built something similar at a low level in Shropshire so he knew it worked. He applied the same principles here but he just took things a little higher. As a sealant he came up with a gasket that was Welsh flannel dipped in boiling sugar and then sealed the edges off with lead. So in real layman's terms, Telford's answer was to build a big tin bath held together with toffee. But it has lasted this long and it hasn't leaked so he got something right.

At a staggering 126 feet high it's not surprising that it

ABOVE: A true high – a crossing with 'Jones The Boats'.
RIGHT: Setting out to cross Telford's 'Stream through the Skies'.

brings a wobble to some people's knees. You certainly need a head for heights to cross it. As Peter explained, he's seen plenty of people brought to a standstill by its vertigo inducing proportions. Whilst I'd managed to cross it thanks to the comfort of Peter's lovely boat I decided I couldn't come here without actually going across on foot.

Its name might provide you with a bit of a tongue twister and its height can also tie your stomach in knots, but one thing is very clear. This 'Stream through the Skies' is a phenomenal piece of engineering. It rubs shoulders with the likes of Stonehenge and the Taj Mahal as a World Heritage Site but it also remains Telford's great legacy, a grand plan on a grand scale that's never since been repeated. What he so brilliantly managed to achieve was to find a way to take the water from the River Dee 6 miles upstream and made it fly above itself here, 126 feet above the river.

It's this bridge which brings so many people to this part of Wales. Walking across it you really can see why so many people come here to gaze and gasp. It really does deserve admiration. But what I've realised is there is so much more to

this tranquil little spot than you might think. This might be the big prize, but back down in the valley there is an unfolding story of a river and a canal and how together, the two helped pave the fortunes of this very lovely green valley.

Ruabon is the nearest railway station and from here its a 10-15 minute taxi ride to Llangollen. If you are travelling by car the nearest available parking to the start of the walk is just above the Chainbridge Hotel. From the end at the Pontcysllte Aqueduct a local bus service provides services returning to Llangollen or onwards towards Ruabon:
www.bryn-melyn.co.uk
Further details are available from the Llangollen Tourist Information: *www.llangollen.org/en/Travel_Information*
Tel: 01978 861345
Recommended Maps: OS Explorer 256

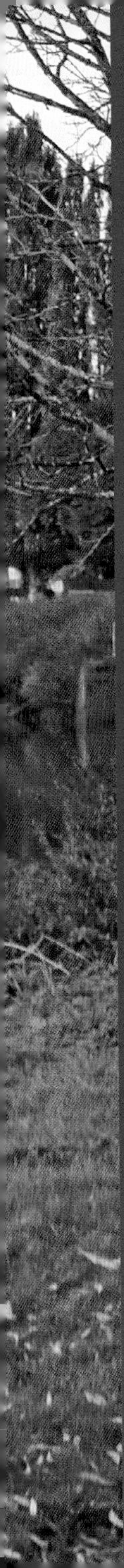

industrial revelations

The Worcester and Birmingham Canal was built to connect the city and the sea and in doing so it changed the fortunes not only of the Midlands but also of the entire country. So this is a tale of two cities and a walk that takes you on a journey from eighteenth century industry to twenty first century escapism.

The city of Worcester by the River Severn.

Worcester's canal network was at the heart of Britain's great industrial age.

history of the canal

The Worcester and Birmingham Canal was designed as a shortcut down to the River Severn and ultimately the ports at Gloucester and Bristol. Digging began in earnest in 1794 and once finished, secured Birmingham's future status as the 'Workshop of the World'. In turn it became known as 'The City of a Thousand Trades' and by 1759 Birmingham was the heart of a manufacturing phenomenon; at least 20,000 people were employed in the production of everything from steam engines and buttons to toys and guns.

According to one industry leader of the time, this success was down to the 'super activity' of the people. But this wasn't the only factor. By the 1790s 'Canal Mania' was born and these new transport superhighways crucially accelerated the delivery of raw materials and the distribution of goods.

The Worcester and Birmingham Canal was to play a crucial role in transforming not simply the geography

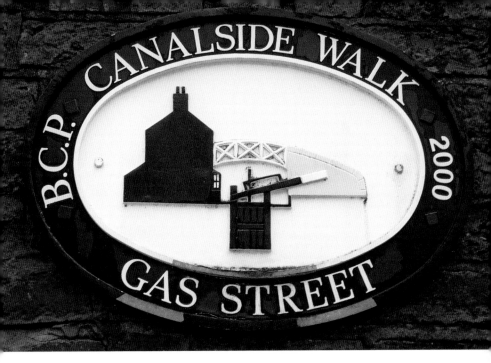

Gas Street Basin marks the start of the walk.

but the landscape in every sense from economics to job prospects. An example of this transformation came in the form of Tardebigge Locks. The longest flight in the UK, it is the impressive half way marker on my walk. The arrival of the Worcester and Birmingham Canal supported an era of formidable industrial activity. This walk allows you discover some of these 'industrial revelations'.

WORCESTER AND BIRMINGHAM CANAL

BIRMINGHAM

GAS STREET BASIN

M 5

M 42

N

RIVER SEVERN

DROITWICH

REDDITCH

A 448

TARDEBIGGE LOCKS

WORCESTER

A 38

THE WALK

Birmingham to the River Severn at Worcester
30 miles/48.2 kilometres

OVERVIEW

This walk can be tackled in a number of ways. For those seeking a more serious physical endeavour, this 30 mile route provides a challenging one-day walk. I tackled it over two days, dividing it into two fifteen mile stretches. What I like about this approach is that you could make a weekend of it. That's really the beauty of these towpath trails, they lend themselves to tackling as much or as little as you might want. There's usually a conveniently located café or pub too.

Quite unlike any of my previous walks, this one starts in the heart of the city and finds its way out into beautiful Worcestershire countryside. After Tardebigge Locks, the towpath leads to another great city of the Midlands, Worcester, birthplace of arguably the greatest ever British composer, Edward Elgar, and home to the world famous Royal porcelain. Here you reach journey's end at lock number one where the canal meets the River Severn. It's certainly a walk of contrasts, as well as a tale of two cities that were at the heart of the golden era of British industry

DAY 1

Gas Street Basin, Birmingham to Tardebigge (15 miles)

Gas Street Basin, in the heart of Birmingham's city centre.

I never thought that I'd be sat in the middle of a city centre proclaiming the virtues of its favourable walking conditions. It's just not the territory I ordinarily end up walking in when I make my television programmes, or even when I go off wandering for pleasure. But that's what I loved about this walk. It's full off the unexpected. For example, ask any Brummie and they'll proudly tell you there are more canals here than in Venice.

Now, technically that's true, but this walk isn't about gondolas or ice cream. This is a walk which plants you firmly in the golden era of the nineteenth century when this city and its canal network was the epicentre of our industrial revolution.

Before I embarked on my journey I had the chance to meet Graham Fisher MBE, canal author and expert as well as a true boy from the 'Black Country'. He's someone who lives and breathes canals, so who better to help set me straight on what lay ahead.

As Graham explained, there are at least eight different canals starting here, all with their own attributes and stories to tell. But as he confirmed, The Worcester and Birmingham Canal just seems to tell the lot. 'Whatever you want, whether it's industrial archaeology, nature at its finest, somewhere to walk the dog ... it's hugely significant. It provided a route from Birmingham down to a section of the Severn. It also helped to move goods made in Birmingham outwards to Worcester and stuff from Worcester coming in to Birmingham. Bearing in mind this area of Birmingham, the Black Country, really was the heart of industry at this time, if something wasn't made here, it wasn't made anywhere in the world', he enthused.

There's always something quite special when you find yourself on a walk and there's a moment when the history of the place really comes to life. This was already happening and it was only the start of the walk. Standing with Graham

Reflections over city centre moorings.

amidst the one-time warehouses and industrial store yards we were at the heart of what was once a very different world. Goods manufactured on this spot once found their way across the globe.

What lay ahead was the journey those goods once went on. And Graham couldn't have sold the walk any better. This description is worthy of inclusion here because it might just encourage you to make this journey, a truly great British walk. 'You suddenly burst out of the city environs and you are surrounded by a veritable cacophony of birds, nature, greenery, it's absolutely splendid. By the time you get to the top of Tardebigge Locks and you are looking down on these winding locks over the valley towards the Severn, it will melt your heart.'

Swans find a home on the Worcester & Birmingham Canal.

From the start of this walk it's very clear that canalside development has played a huge part in rejuvenating the city. Over four hundred and eighty eight million pounds has been invested since 2001 and new buildings and apartment blocks abound. That is, until you get to Edgbaston, home not only to the famous cricket ground but also to some of Birmingham's most exclusive residences.

It was the vision of the landowner Sir Henry Gough-Calthorpe in the 1700s, to keep Edgbaston a rural oasis in the heart of an industrial city, free of factories and warehouses. A very attractive proposition for the well-to-do of Birmingham; and Edgbaston became the fashionable place to live for the increasingly prosperous middle classes who wanted to escape the stench, smoke and noise.

The Cadbury factory, home of the famous chocolate.

But in 1791 an act of parliament granted the Worcester and Birmingham Canal Company the authority to cut a waterway through Sir Henry's estate. Objections to the impact of the canal meant the project dragged on for twenty four years, with a host of different engineers all putting their name to it. It also took time to finalise the design because the water supply to the mills had to be protected too. The arrival of the canal couldn't compromise this. The solution was to build narrower locks to minimise demands on local water.

Sir Henry had clout in parliament and he made sure there could be no towpaths, no warehouses and no wharves on the same side as the stately homes. And on top of that, the landed gentry could transport all of their own goods

In the 1870s, Cadbury moved from grimy industrial Birmingham with the trailblazing vision of creating a workers' paradise. Richard and George Cadbury spent their Sundays strolling the green fields to the south of the city trying to find a suitable spot next to the canal to escape the terrible slums of the inner city. Bournville was the result – not only the base for their factory but the first planned community in the world, a 'model village' with shops, churches, schools, reading rooms and hospitals.

For forty years, up until the 1920s, the factory enjoyed a full working relationship with the canal, bringing in raw materials like cocoa beans from as far away as Ghana and shipping their famous chocolate to the colonies. But even as the train arrived and use of the canal declined, it was still used on a minor domestic scale by the factory right into the 1960s. You may well wish to linger a little longer, then follow your nose to Cadbury World, a state of the art exhibition which allows you to explore and discover more about this iconic chocolate's history. And at least you'll get to do some tasting.

for free and were granted full fishing rights. Clearly being powerful had its benefits.

But it does mean that today's Birmingham has a lovely place to escape within the city limits. As you continue south towards the outskirts of Birmingham you approach a station with a very familiar name – Bournville. And from the canal you can spy the Cadbury factory. Its position there suggests that back in the day it must have had some connection to the canal. But at the time of filming the more immediate and pressing question for me was how could the producers of this programme bring me so close to a chocolate factory and not let me go inside! To make matters worse, a quick sniff of the air – I'm not lying, it smelt of chocolate!

For me however, the towpath beckoned south. As those

TOP: *Signpost at Gas Street Basin.*
BOTTOM: *The Worcester and Birmingham Canal.*

lovely smells diminish, Birmingham finally fades into the distance and the canal disappears into a one and a half mile tunnel. Unfortunately, there's no towpath, which means going overground just like the boat horses used to. Horses proved their worth in the days of canal transportation, hauling loads of up to fifty tonnes. Although back in the day donkeys were often favoured here because they were small enough to hop on board and save time by being able to go through the tunnel rather than over it.

No such luck for us walkers, and the route diverts through Hawkesley and a housing estate built in the 1970s after Birmingham's inner slums were cleared. A mile on however, and you are in rural Worcestershire. Once back on the towpath, on the other side of the tunnel, it's a very different scene. The canal now nestles beneath a canopy of high trees surrounded by rolling green countryside.

After just over eight miles of this lovely easy going walking the route passes the quaint little village of Alvechurch. This sleepy hollow was birthplace of author Fay Weldon as well as Godfrey Baseley, creator of *The Archers*, the longest running radio broadcast anywhere in the world. It was the surrounding Worcestershire countryside that was supposed to have inspired his rural soap opera.

The towpath eases gently along for another six miles or so to the half way point on my walk where a beautiful eighteenth century church spire up on the hill announces the village of Tardebigge. Here, it's well worth heading up on to the bridge to really soak up this charming view, a lovely reward at the end of day one.

DAY 2

From Tardebigge to the River Severn, Worcester (15 miles)

Tardebigge Bottom Lock.

Day two certainly gets off to a dramatic start. Tardebigge Locks lie ahead, a dramatic two mile flight of locks, lowering the canal 220 feet. You start at lock 58 and as you drop downhill so do the numbers. Descending the whole flight takes you to lock 29. Lock number one is still another 15 miles away, the prize at the end of the walk, when you finally get to Worcester.

This is also where the author of a surprise bestseller moored up during the bleak years of World War II. Tom Rolt's book, *Narrow Boat*, written in 1944, documents the story of his travels with his wife along what remained of the decaying canals.

To his surprise, it was a resounding hit with both the public and critics. Not least, it seemed to appeal to national pride and the determination to preserve Britain's heritage. At the end of the book, he writes:

'But if the canals are left to the mercies of economists and scientific planners, before many years are past the last of them will become a weedy stagnant ditch and the bright boats will rot at the wharves, to live on only in old men's memories.'

A puzzled Tom Rolt was inundated with fan mail. One letter that caught his attention was from another young writer, Robert Aickman, who shared his love for canals. In it, he proposed the formation of a society to revive Britain's neglected canal network. But that's not the only thing that makes this part of the canal special.

What's surprising when you get here is that you suddenly realise a whole fifteen miles of canal have gone already and there hasn't actually been a lock. The terrain at Tardebigge presented a major geographical obstacle for the canal builders. The route so far had travelled from Birmingham on a plateau, but here the canal needed to descend.

The initial solution incorporated twelve boatlifts that would move boats up and down this section. Because of worries

Julia at Stoke Bottom Lock.

about the cost of such an elaborate scheme, only one was built and the great canal engineer John Rennie was drafted in to assess the plan. He concluded that it would not survive the rough treatment it would receive from the boatmen and so the boatlift was abandoned in favour of the locks we see today.

At lock 57 you pass the old engine house which used to help maintain water levels in the canal. When it takes an average ninety thousand gallons of water every time the lock gates open, you realise why the canal engineers needed to stockpile water close by. Tardebigge Reservoir continues to keep this flight of locks in action with feeder channels now directing water back into the canal. It's right next to the towpath so you can quickly hop up for a change of view. After that it's simply lock after lock after lock flowing downwards – a truly lovely sight indeed.

Negotiating this flight of locks is considered to be a rite of passage by boaters. It's definitely one for the tick list. Britain's canals are packed with the technological wonders of their

Canal cottages line the towpath.

day. But of all the surprising engineering feats this has surely got to be one of the most impressive.

By this point in my walk it definitely felt like time for a cuppa and I met lockkeeper Alan Troth and his wife Barbara at lock 18, where they live right next to the canal. As we sat outside their house enjoying the view of bustling boats and busy locks it became increasingly obvious that getting through these locks maybe isn't quite as easy as it looked. Alan then laid down the gauntlet: 'C'mon Julia come and have a go'. Never one to resist a challenge, it was time to roll back the fleece and show what I was made of. I pushed, I leaned, I heaved and eventually I got the lock gate turning but it was still a long way from Barbara's cheery announcement that she could do it with one hand. Nothing like being well

Canal near Stoke Prior.

and truly put in your place. I can definitely confirm for those thinking of taking the narrowboat option along the canal, it's not the easy option. Just trying to do this once was hard work enough, never mind the fifty eight times that boaters face.

Stepping back on the towpath I found myself thinking how much the history of this canal still felt like it was alive. Alan & Barbara's lovely little cottage, dating back to 1850, has been home to generations of lockkeepers just like them, doing the same jobs as them and passing on these simple canal traditions and skills. Their home was one of the remaining symbols of the heyday of the canal, when goods like chocolate crumb and coal were carried past its front door. Today, the scene hasn't changed all that much. Traffic continues and at least three thousand boats chug by each year. But rather than goods, these narrowboats are carrying passengers enjoying their holidays.

The walk is now focussed on the final home straight and the goal of Worcester, once the heart of Britain's porcelain making business and home to Edward Elgar (as well as that eponymous sauce).

But apart from the canal, very little is left today of Worcester's manufacturing past. Gone are the big factories and warehouses which made use of the canal and its link to the nearby River Severn. The Worcester Porcelain Museum is one of the few remaining clues that there was ever a formidable industry here. I was able to meet its curator Wendy Cook to retrace some of that history.

Standing on the quiet secluded stretch of towpath, Wendy pointed out the former factory buildings, where four large kilns once stood. Today, it's a tranquil spot amidst urban development. It's hard to imagine that Worcester was once an industrial centre which by the mid 1870s had four factories producing fantastic porcelain for the best customers that was shipped all over the world, from America to India and even as far away as China.

Before the canal, manufacturing had to rely on goods being brought up the nearby River Severn and then transported via a muddy packhorse track, which was time-consuming as well as risky. The finished products were delicate, breakable and often heavy. The canal provided a simple method to move these goods along and in turn allowed the industry to expand and to produce even more porcelain.

Today, the site of one of those factories lines the towpath and is being converted into des res apartments. It's great to see this giving a new lease of life to the buildings and this part of the town.

The final stretch of the canal is only half a mile and whilst it's only a short section, it's not hard to see how it would have

The rolling Worcesteshire countryside.

transformed business in Worcester. It was this little bit of canal that swiftly linked to the Severn and the world beyond and was used commercially right up until the 1960s.

It's been quite a journey for me too, from landlocked Birmingham high up on a plateau, down to sea level and my final goal, the first lock of the canal. And this is where my waterway joins an even bigger one, the River Severn. Should you even need reminding just how far you've walked there's a perfectly positioned signpost announcing 'Birmingham 30 miles, 58 locks'.

Lock 1 finally opened its gates in December 1815 to a display of canon fire and music as a hopeful and expectant crowd cheered the first passage of boats. Within two weeks the exchange of cargo was in full flow between the canal and river, with everything from china clay to cocoa beans being transported up and down the waterways.

The Worcester and Birmingham Canal embodies the story of the industrial revolution: without canals, manufacturing

The Worcestershire countryside inspired much of Edward Elgar's work.

couldn't have grown the way it did. Ironically, today they serve as an escape from modern life. People live by them, walk alongside them, and cycle on their towpaths. They fit into the countryside like any river or stream, and in towns and cities they're a tranquil haven. Bet the canal builders didn't expect that.

Birmingham and Worcester are both well served by national rail and bus connections.
Details on travelling to Birmingham are available from Visit Birmingham; *www.visitbirmingham.com*
For more information on getting to and from Worcester consult the travel pages of Visit Worcester:
www.visitworcester.com/how_to_get_here.asp
Recommended maps: OS Explorer 220 & 204

from coast to coast

This is a walk that takes you to the dramatic west coast of Scotland where mountains meet the sea. It's not only a walk through a wild and dramatic landscape but also a walk through early nineteenth century history when Thomas Telford transformed these remote Highlands by creating a 'coast to coast' canal that linked east to west.

Telford was one of the great engineers of his day. On the outskirts of Fort William is his most ambitious project, the Caledonian Canal. In the early 1800s he realised there was a way through the heart of this remote and inhospitable region. By following the Great Glen, one of Scotland's most dramatic natural features, he saw that he could link its freshwater lochs with sections of manmade canal. But there had never been a canal route on this scale before. Telford truly had his work cut out if he was to conquer the Highlands. More than a simple story of canal building, it's a tale of fame, fortune and ultimately folly. This wasn't just a navigational short cut.

The view to Fort William from the Caledonian Canal.

CALEDONIAN

ABOVE: Neptune's Staircase at Banavie.
RIGHT: Julia on the Moy Swing Bridge in the heart of the Highlands.

history of the canal

Telford spent two years surveying the options for this route and returned a compelling report to the government.

The devastating Highland Clearances had shattered traditional clan life; people were being evicted from their homes and forced off their land to make way for sheep farming. Dispossessed and disillusioned they were leaving Scotland, emigrating to the 'New World' and the promise of a better life. Telford, a Scot, believed the canal could give his fellow countrymen a reason to stay. He wrote:

'From the best information I have been able to produce, about three thousand persons went away in the course of the last year and if I am rightly informed, three times that number are preparing to leave the country in the present year. A canal would not only create much needed employment, it would also be hugely beneficial to the fishing industry, providing jobs way beyond the canal's completion.'

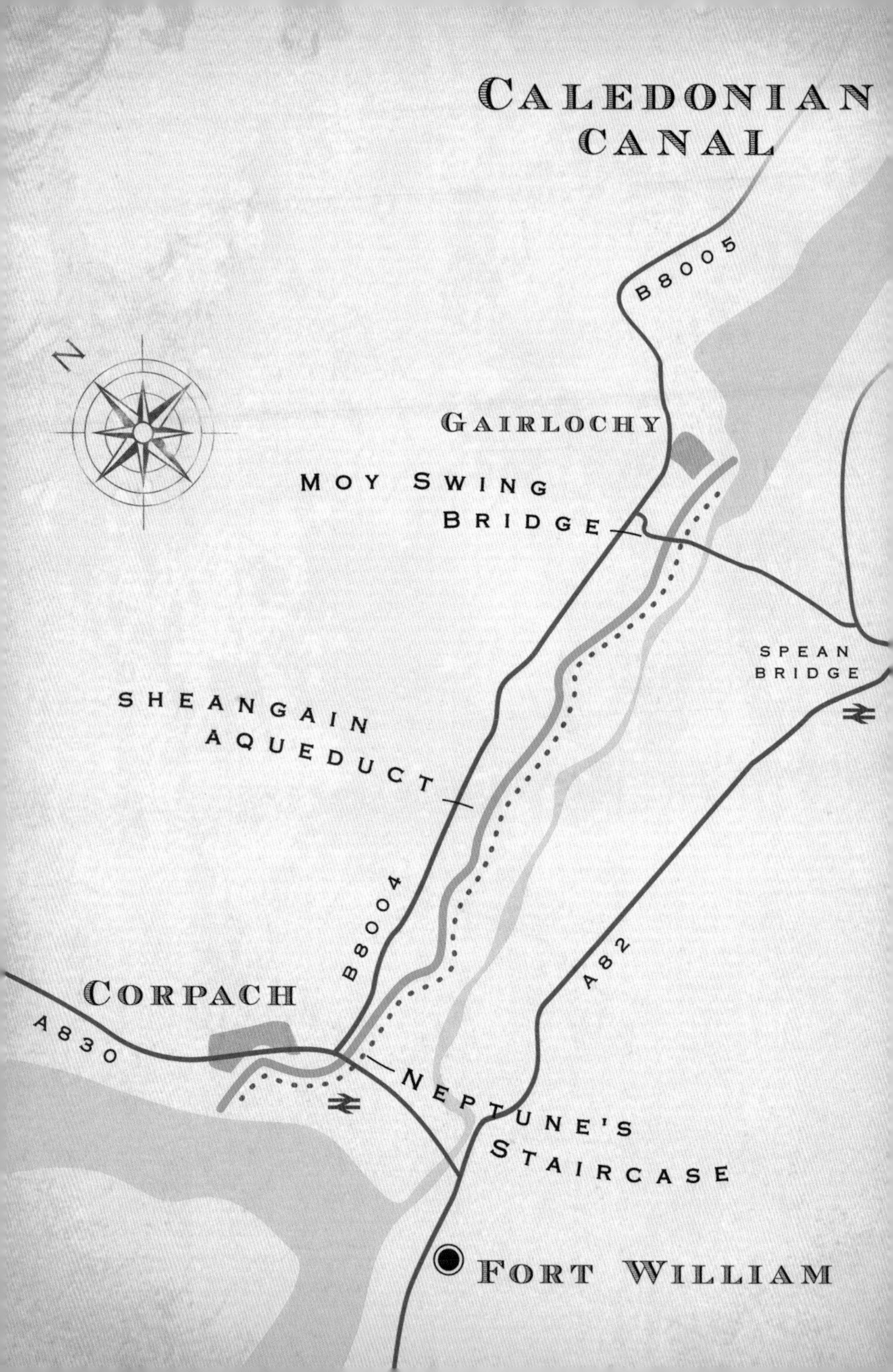

CALEDONIAN CANAL

B8005

GAIRLOCHY

MOY SWING BRIDGE

SPEAN BRIDGE

SHEANGAIN AQUEDUCT

B8004

A82

CORPACH

A830

NEPTUNE'S STAIRCASE

● FORT WILLIAM

THE WALK

From Corpach Sea Lock to Loch Lochy

8 miles / 12.8 kilometres

OVERVIEW

By the turn of the nineteenth century 'Canal Mania' was well underway in the industrial heartlands of England. But it wasn't until 1801 that Telford started to survey a new route that would change the face of Scotland. Telford saw that the four main lochs of the Great Glen, including Loch Ness, the largest and deepest in the UK, lay in near perfect alignment across the north of Scotland. Building an additional 22 miles of manmade canal would link them and create a cross-country route between Fort William and Inverness. This walk follows the first eight miles of the 60 mile route. It starts by the sea at Corpach and ends on the shores of the first freshwater loch at Gairlochy.

STAGE 1

Corpach Sea Lock to Neptune's Staircase

Corpach Sea Lock and the start of the walk.

This is a walk which starts with a bang. Corpach Sea Lock is the start (or end) point of a journey along the Caledonian Canal and it guards the entrance to Loch Linnhe and the open sea beyond. Mountains drape the edges and when the mist is low and the clouds racing, it's truly a 'bonny' and dramatic view. It doesn't take long in these surroundings to realise that this is not your average canal and that some of the boats passing through are not your average narrowboats.

My TV walk certainly got off to an interesting start when we came face to face with one of these very big canal boats. The impressive and unmissable 'Lord of the Glens' is a cruise boat for 54 passengers, which ploughs the length of the canal in about four days and continues on to the Inner Hebridean islands. I was able to intercept its captain, Anthony Reading to find out whether this really was all plain sailing.

He explained that this is the largest vessel that will fit into the locks of the Caledonian and that there's often only one or two feet either end and in the smaller locks only about 18 inches either end. It really looked a tight squeeze. But then Telford clearly didn't anticipate a cruise ship of tourists when he first made his plans. He had other ideas.

Telford's plan to join two sides of the country via a waterway was definitely a bold one. At the time there was nothing of its scale anywhere else in the UK. But for Telford this wasn't simply another canal to add to his portfolio. Born in Dumfriesshire in 1757, Telford might have been a Lowlander but he was still a Scot. For this pioneering and patriotic engineer the canal was also a matter of national pride. He pledged the canal would bring prosperity and employment to the impoverished Highlands and help fishing boats shortcut the Pentland Firth, the treacherous route round the top of Scotland.

In England and Wales, canal building had already taken hold and private speculators had rushed forwards to fund new schemes in order to expand Britain's transport network. But this route was different; for the first time ever the government would provide the money. If successful, it would be a triumph of its age, the country's first 'social enterprise scheme' which Telford described as 'one of the noblest projects that was ever laid before a nation'. He was determined to overcome all barriers.

Setting out from Corpach I could still find the tell tale signs of Telford's grand ambition. A couple of chunky and substantial looking sea-faring tugs were moored up, a clear reminder that Telford's massive shipping canal was on an unprecedented scale, making it capable of carrying these ocean-going boats. I'd come to expect colourful narrowboats, with their cosy puffing chimneys and smell of woodsmoke. Not here. Things were going to be different in this wild, cross-country glen.

LEFT: Treading the towpath on the Caledonian Canal.
ABOVE: Corpach Double Lock.

As the walk gets going up through the next double locks it's not hard to see the kinds of obstacles that stood in the way of Telford's pioneering mind. This is true mountain country. Ben Nevis, the tallest mountain in Great Britain, is clearly visible, towering over the town of Fort William. But Telford wasn't put off. He planned a route that sliced through the dramatic faultline of the Great Glen, 20 feet deep, 30 feet wide with a total of 28 gargantuan locks. Imagine being audacious enough to think you could dig a canal through this terrain. I mean, even on the Telford scale this was off the chart.

After just under a mile the walk arrives at the edges of the village of Banavie. Carving a canal through these giant mountains was an astonishing challenge that ended up going massively over budget and took much longer than ever planned. I was able to meet Nigel Rix, a modern day engineer who works for British Waterways, the organisation responsible for the upkeep of these waterways and someone who could tell me a little bit more about Telford's Highland mission.

Nigel is someone who is also a clear ambassador, fan and fountain of facts when it came to all things Caledonian Canal. So it was with infectious enthusiasm that he was able to remind me that at the time of its building in the early nineteenth century (1803-1822), this was the largest canal of its kind. There was nothing like it in Britain at all. As Nigel explained, 'It was simply massive, a huge ship canal, as opposed to a small canal like those down in England. It was beyond the imagination really'.

I was also really keen to find out a bit more about how this great scheme came to life; where did the cash come from? Again Nigel reiterated that what also makes this canal so special is that for the first time ever it was funded, not by private speculators keen to capitalise, but instead by a government keen to find an answer to the mass unemployment and emigration problems. The controversial Highland Clearances meant many people in this area had lost their homes and their livelihoods. Telford's idea for a cross-country canal provided an answer, with a kind of 'nationalised' job creation scheme. So, it was a master plan that covered all bases.

Talking to Nigel I began to see Thomas Telford as more than simply a civil engineer doing his job. With this canal in particular there seemed to be a deep-rooted concern for the future of his fellow countrymen. The canal could provide an answer that would help secure a future for the country, providing employment and also enhancing trade and transport. Nigel was emphatic about this: 'He was a genius. He was a great visionary. He was so enthusiastic that when he started he actually began six months before he got the signature on the bit of paper. They had to rein him back. He was so enthusiastic, so keen'.

Just a short walk along the canal beyond the Banavie Rail Bridge is perhaps the greatest example of Telford's genius at work on this canal, the start of Neptune's Staircase, a dramatic flight of locks. It was named after Neptune, the Roman god of

Neptune's Staircase, a dramatic flight of eight locks.

the seas, by the 'navvies' – the name given to the men who 'navigated' the route and built it. In an impressive staircase of eight locks, the canal rises 64 feet in 450 yards. Again, at the time of building there was nothing else like it.

Without this dramatic feature the canal simply wouldn't have worked. We are in the Highlands after all and surrounded by some pretty lofty mountains. Put simply, water doesn't travel up. This was Telford's simple solution, allowing the canal to navigate the height gain at this section. It's the largest section of locks on the whole canal and today it takes boats about an hour and a half to go through. What it means of course is that you have a little climb on your hands. Not something you normally expect on a canal walk.

Neptune's Staircase might provide us walkers with a bit of a challenge but it also proved to be an obstacle for shipping. On 22 February 1929, the boat, 'Girl Patricia' crashed through the top lock and was then swept into the next, damaging its gates, before being brought to a stop. The sudden increase in water pressure then threatened the southern wall. If it had collapsed all the water in this reach could have cascaded down, flooding the village of Banavie. That's what I call a close thing.

STAGE 2

Neptune's Staircase to Loy Sluices

Approaching Loy Sluices.

Now, whenever I go and film my walks there's always one thing that can scupper all our best-laid plans. And that 'thing', lurking in the background, is the weather. So whenever the words 'it's probably a bit of waterproofs day today' are uttered by the producer ... well, you know what you're in for. I've certainly had my fair share of showers throughout my walks and the Caledonian looked intent on showing me no relief. This was definitely a walk of contrasts in the truest sense. From showers to sunshine, mountains to wooded slopes, there is a bit of everything. But the waterproofs were packed. I was armed and ready, although my poor cameraman Jan probably could have done with a few more dry lens cloths. But as he kept saying, 'you don't get magical light without a bit of pain'. I think it was through gritted teeth.

For most canals built in England, securing a constant supply of water was an issue. Not here in Scotland. In fact it was the opposite; there could often be too much water. Heavy rain meant that flooding could easily threaten the banks of the canal (and yes I can vouch for the fact that it definitely rains here on the west coast). By planting an embankment of half a million trees with spruces from Sweden, and 20,000 fine thorns, Telford strengthened the banks against the potentially devastating rising waters.

After leaving Neptune's Staircase you make your way along a lovely tree-lined corridor, the end result of Telford's clever bank strengthening mission. But planting trees wasn't enough to secure the canal. Telford needed to implement some of the tricks of the trade he'd been developing elsewhere on some of his other canal projects. After just over two miles a rather inconspicuous aqueduct lies hidden below the towpath. If you look carefully you'll find a little sign for the Shengain Aqueduct, which directs you off down a steepish little track. Head down here and you'll be able to see

LEFT: *Telford's tree-lined towpath.*
RIGHT: *The view of the Loy Sluices from below.*
OPPOSITE: *The Shengain Aqueduct.*

more clearly how this structure carries the towpath and the canal across it. Here I bumped into Ian MacLaren, the man responsible for looking after the upkeep of this very dinky little structure.

Ian was midway through drain maintenance work but he agreed to give me a little guided tour. We walked though the archway (which also provides road access to people living either side of the canal) and halfway along I suddenly seemed to gather my bearings and realised that I was actually now stood directly underneath the canal. As Ian explained, there were tonnes of water now passing over my head, nearly 20 feet of water. The aqueduct enabled water to be channelled off the mountains and stop it from flooding into the canal. So this little structure, nearly two hundred years old, acts as a kind of drainage system as well; another one of Telford's

masterstrokes. Ian was there to make sure the aqueduct could continue to serve its humble but still important role. And as I learned, he came from a family of long standing canal workers. He was the fourth generation to have worked on this canal, which totted up to over 120 years of service from one family. As we parted company Ian joked 'I'm afraid British Waterways have had the whole of our family and that's us I think'. Fair enough. I think the Maclarens have shown their fair share of dedication.

Back up on the towpath Telford's lovely thick tree-lined embankment continues, making for some easy going and scenic walking. But eventually the trees give way to an altogether more Highland scene. This is where you get a real sense of the truly mountainous terrain Telford had to pioneer a route through. Look out for the little gap that opens up on your right hand side and you should be able to see the back of Ben Nevis and to its left a little hut over on Aonach Mor, which is at the top of the cable car and represents the ski industry in this area. The great thing about this walk is

ABOVE: The Caledonian Canal cuts through the heart of the Great Glen.
RIGHT: The towpath runs parallel to the River Loy.

that you don't just have mountains at the start, they are with you every step of the way. And for those of us who love our mountains this is a particularly appealing walk. You feel like you really are in the heart of the hills.

In this mountainous landscape Telford had to be prepared for just how much rain could pour off these slopes. Building aqueducts and strengthening the banks weren't his only precautions. He also needed to have a way of letting water out of the canal should it simply get too full. After another mile or so you discover Telford's answer – the Loy Sluices; an overflow system that would allow water to be drained from the canal through a sluice gate. Again a little scramble down from the towpath and you can peer over the sturdy stone wall which guards the structure below. On the day of my walk the pool below was like a millpond, calm and serene. So the sluice gate was shut, the plug was well and truly in.

STAGE 3

Loy Sluices to Loch Lochy

Approaching the only swing bridge left on the canal.

Telford might have had the answers to some of the engineering problems which the route posed, but he knew these would amount to nothing without a strong and dedicated workforce. To cut the canal line alone required the removal of five and a quarter million cubic yards of soil. This would have been such incredibly arduous work with only a barrow, a pickaxe and brute force.

Just a short walk from the Loy Sluices, look out for the information board tucked to the side of the towpath. It shows an impressionistic drawing of just what it must have been like for the navvies here, trying to dig a route through this wild landscape. This must have been tough, dirty, physical work. It also mentions that they had a 'pernicious habit' of drinking whisky. Well, I'm not surprised, I mean you'd need something to help you through a day like that!

These Highland labourers were more used to working in isolation as subsistence crofters than in teams of hundreds. Many proved unreliable, returning to their crofts during certain seasons to take part in peat cutting and harvesting. Telford's grand plan started to falter. His survey hadn't accurately estimated the costs of cutting locks through rock and the seven year deadline proved unrealistic. Instead it was to take a total of nineteen years.

But Telford's route through the Great Glen has paved the way for one of the country's most popular long distance walking trails. This 73 mile route now attracts walkers intent on the challenge of crossing the country on foot. The route between Fort William and Inverness is slightly longer than Telford's canal and takes about six days to complete. So whenever you see the wooden markers with the thistle then think of all those walkers who are now treading in Telford's footsteps.

There's one more unmissable feature on the canal coming up. I was lucky enough to meet the man with the rather lovely job of 'winding' his way on this canal. Ivor Mackay is the Moy Swing Bridge operator. Now, like me, you might ask why does a bridge need an operator? Well, Moy Swing Bridge is no ordinary bridge.

This two hundred year old bridge is the only swing bridge on the canal and it's still performing the same job as when it was first built. The canal only got the go ahead to carve its path through this section if the farmer could still access his farmland either side. The answer was a bridge that, to this day, needs to be left closed for the farmer to cross whenever he wishes. Ivor's job is to open it for any passing boats. In the height of summer this can be as many as twenty a day. The original bridge keeper would have lived in the little white house opposite. Ivor explained that he had a window in each gable end so that even when he was in bed he would be able to see boats coming through. If you go to the eastern end of the house you can still make one out.

Seeing Ivor's bridge in 'full swing' is a great reminder of just how much care goes into the canal's up-keep, which today has the impressive title of being a 'Scheduled Ancient Monument' and is also set to be enjoyed by another generation of boaters as the country's first ever designated canoe trail.

In just a short distance you get your clearest view of the River Loy on your right hand side, which has been burbling alongside throughout our walk. It's been a walk brimming with wild drama and silent sweeping landscapes but sadly it's now the last stretch to the double locks at Gairlochy.

Originally there was only one lock here. But in 1834 heavy rains flooded three feet above the lock gates, threatening the entire western section. For two days and two nights the lockkeepers worked around the clock to stem this growing tide. They built emergency turf dams and all the sluices were opened wide. It was a telling warning.

One lock was not enough. A second was added in 1844,

LEFT: Arriving at Gairlochy Bottom Lock.
RIGHT: An old anchor lines the towpath at Gairlochy.

the only lock on the canal which doesn't date from the original construction.

Not everything went to plan for Telford. The canal finally opened in 1822, twelve years later than planned, costing over £905,000 rather than the £350,000 he predicted. By the time it was finished, advances in shipping had made the north coast more navigable and boats didn't need the canal shortcut. Despite a slight reprieve during both World Wars for munitions shipping, commercial activity never really took off. But the canal has a new life now. People are enjoying it on boats, on bikes, in boots, all sorts.

Today it's the tourist industry that takes up the story and the canal attracts over half a million visitors each year. So just as Telford intended, the Highlands are prospering – all thanks to his canal, which connected these lochs and created a gateway into the magnificent scenery of the Great Glen.

After you leave the locks at Gairlochy it doesn't take too long before you get your first view of Loch Lochy, which

LEFT: The final stretch of canal before Loch Lochy.
RIGHT: Peaceful moorings at Gairlochy.

Telford so cleverly realised could be part of a connecting chain, forging a route through this wild cross-country valley. It's an impressive view indeed of the Great Glen where the mountains plunge dramatically on either side to its shore. It's definitely a place to pause and reflect on what a journey it's been, from saltwater to a freshwater loch.

Your final marker is the lighthouse, which guides shipping between canal and loch. It watches over a view worth savouring. Loch and mountains stretch almost seamlessly in front of you, uncluttered, uncomplicated and simply beautiful. This will feel like a real reward at the end of a thoroughly satisfying walk.

With this canal Telford created something on a scale that had never been seen before. You can't fail to be impressed and yet it became a bit of a white elephant. It took three times as long to build, it went over budget and it was never fully utilised. But he did realise a dream, an enormous dream, he changed the local economy and that still resonates today. What an exquisite walk, what a legacy.

End goal: Loch Lochy. From seawater to freshwater.

Fort William is the nearest railway station. From here you can follow the first section of the Great Glen Way to the start of the canal at Corpach (approx 15-20 minute walk). Alternatively local taxi companies provide drop-off and collection services. For more information: *www.visit-fortwilliam.co.uk/fort-william-travel-information-and-travel-services*

Recommended maps: OS Explorer 400, 392

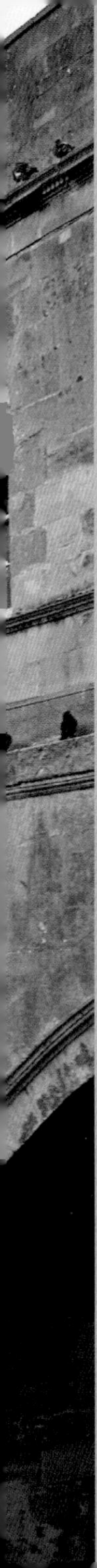

restoration & renaissance

A tale of two halves, the rise and fall and then rise again of this grand canal makes for a varied and beautiful walk. This canal has certainly been full of surprising history. It's been a nineteenth century superhighway, a derelict ditch, a desperate last line of defence for a nation under possible attack, and now a leisure park that's also home to hundreds seeking an alternative way of living.

This is a walk with a powerful tale to tell of restoration, resistance and renaissance.

Pulteney Bridge on the River Avon, Bath.

history of the canal

Two hundred years ago this was a hub of industrialisation. With no reliable roads at the time, only mud tracks, the Kennet and Avon Canal was opened in 1810 to provide a valuable trade link between Bristol and London. When this route got the go ahead from Parliament it was 1793 and 'Canal Mania' was at its height. Buoyed by the success of canal builders in the Midlands, speculators saw that they could expect as much as a 50% return on their investment. The Kennet & Avon secured 750 investors and £420,000, £13.5 milion in today's money.

But with the arrival of trains this landscape was changed forever. The railway lines slowly started to take the traffic

The impressive Caen Hill lock flight.
LEFT: Julia takes a break in Bath on the Kennet & Avon Canal.

from the canal and it began to fall into disuse. By 1950 this canal was not operating and was in a sorry state of disrepair. At this point, a movement to get canals open again was spreading across the country. The Kennet and Avon Canal Trust was formed in 1962 to 'protect, enhance and promote' the canal. After years of backbreaking volunteer work, in 1996 the Trust, together with British Waterways and the local council, secured a Heritage Lottery Fund Grant of a staggering £25 million, the largest sum ever awarded. It was this surge of cash which allowed the Trust to get the canal back into the fabulous condition we see today.

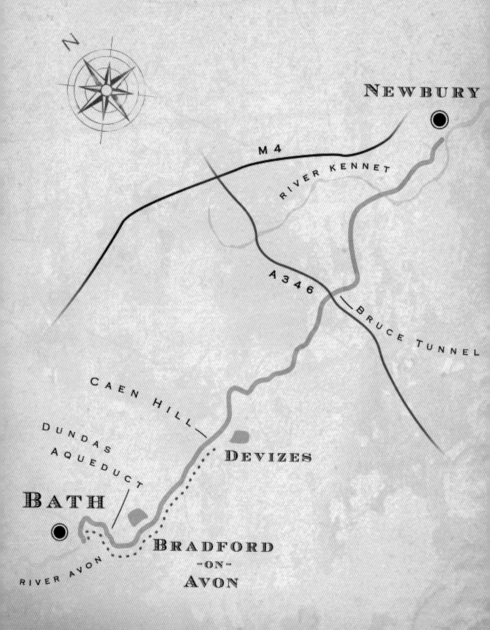

Kennet and Avon Canal

N

NEWBURY

M 4

RIVER KENNET

A 346

BRUCE TUNNEL

CAEN HILL

DUNDAS
AQUEDUCT

DEVIZES

BATH

BRADFORD
-on-
AVON

RIVER AVON

THE WALK

From Bath to Caen Hill Lock Flight

20 miles / 32.18 kilometres

OVERVIEW

This walk follows what is arguably the most picturesque part of the canal as it curves its way round the Avon Valley, shoulder to shoulder with the river. After reaching the half-way point at Bradford-on-Avon the course straightens out as it heads toward Devizes, finishing at the top of the breathtaking Caen Hill flight of locks, a significant engineering achievement and one of the seven listed 'Wonders of British Waterways'.

STAGE 1

Bath to Bathampton

The River Avon provides a link to the Kennet & Avon Canal.

The walk starts impressively, in the World Heritage city of Bath in Somerset. It was the Georgians who turned this place into a luxury spa resort, quite literally 'fit enough for a king'. But this route allows you to explore its other water attraction.

You begin in the heart of the city at Pulteney Bridge, an eighteenth century creation reminiscent of Florence's Ponte Vecchio. It's also, intriguingly, one of only four bridges in the world with shops across the full span on both sides. It's the River Avon which flows beneath its graceful arches and then plunges over the tiered Pulteney Weir. Keeping it on your right you briefly head south following its course to an inconspicuous entrance and the start of another of Britain's great waterways. This was a 'canal superhighway' linking two of the country's most important ports – Bristol and London.

The restored pump house over on the left-hand-side is a clue to the first engineering challenge which the canal builders faced two hundred years ago. They had to keep the canal supplied with water as it climbed up the steep Avon Valley ahead. This means a bit of an uphill walk to begin with, going along a succession of six beautifully restored locks, rising 65 feet to the rooftops of Bath.

Here, you can't help but notice how the buildings make use of a distinctive honey coloured stone. This unmistakable building material was actually formed over 135 million years ago when Bath was under a shallow sea. But it was the Romans who established the city in AD 43 and first discovered its hot springs, the only ones occurring naturally in the whole of the UK. It wasn't until the eighteenth century that Bath took off as a spa resort, leaving this legacy of exemplary Georgian architecture crafted from the city's distinctive stone. Today, this waterway might provide city centre escapism but surprisingly it nearly went to rack and ruin.

The towpath leads you upwards to the rooftops of Bath.

I had the chance to meet Mike Rodd, from the Kennet & Avon Canal Trust, the charity which tirelessly fought to bring the canal back from near extinction. We met in a lovely, picturesque spot, close to Bath Top Lock but as I was to learn it hasn't always been that way. Mike described how in the 1950s the canal was in a sad state of 'total desolation' and how the Trust was formed 'to get the waterway open again, get boaters going through it and also to celebrate the wonderful history that's all around you where there are some really precious buildings over two hundred years old'.

Meeting Mike at the start of my walk was also perfect timing for a bit of advice on what to look out for on my journey ahead. If Mike's description was anything to go by I quickly realised that I was in store for a very lovely walk. It promised what Mike passionately described as 'two of the greatest aqueducts in the world'. Mike also added: 'This canal is all about people and the wonderful culture that exists on the canal. One thing that anyone who goes on this canal

The canal takes you through the heart of the city.

soon discovers is that people stop and talk. And it's quite amazing the culture that builds up. There are also people who live on the canal. We've got people who sell things on the canal, there's a lovely little boat that goes up and down selling cheese, there's another guy who brings your coal and your oil to your boat. So there's a fabulous community that has developed'. This canal's got people, it's got history, it's a real survivor. Today it's also a major leisure industry and at least seven million people a year visit in one way or another.

As you continue along the towpath, unbelievably you are still in urban Bath. City life is bustling just beyond these lovely enveloping trees and still waters. The next key marker on the route is an unmistakable building which straddles the canal, called Cleveland House. This was the former headquarters of The Kennet and Avon Canal Company, a twenty four strong management committee, which controlled the 57 mile route from this rather resplendent position.

I'd been reading about a secret little spot tucked away in the roof of the tunnel under the building that reveals a bit more about how canal trade was controlled by the company, and profits were made from levying tolls, so I was keen to see what I could find. With torch in hand I had a little snoop and managed to find the clever little hatch which connected Cleveland House to the waterway so that the boatmen could leave paperwork and money which the clerks could collect on the way through.

But the pursuit of all this wealth and power also carried a price tag for the Canal Company. This next stage of the route needed to forge a path through one of the most exclusive areas of Bath, the lovely Sydney Gardens. To get permission to go through they needed to pay the owners a whopping £2,000, the deal also demanding they build ornate wrought iron bridges for the residents to cross the canal.

LEFT: Julia prepares to enter the Cleveland Tunnel.
RIGHT: Julia enjoys the tranquility of Sydney Gardens, a favourite haunt of Jane Austen.
OPPOSITE: Cleveland House, former headquarters of the Kennet and Avon Canal Company.

Sydney Gardens is Bath's oldest park, a popular 'resort of leisure' for nineteenth century gentry and frequently visited by royalty. It's so evocative of the period. You almost feel like you're in a Jane Austen novel, which isn't surprising because it was actually an old haunt of the author during the years she lived here in Bath. Sydney Gardens also signals the end of one phase of the walk and the start of another. Once you leave the tunnel here you step out into lovely verdant countryside.

STAGE 2

Bathampton to Bradford-on-Avon

Moored houseboats line the towpath.

Already there was a really different feel to this canal. It didn't just have a lovely bustling feel to it, it felt really alive and fresh. There are quirky works of art dotted along it, including things like a recycled bench made from a hollowed tree trunk. It came complete with its own little plaque which read: 'I'd love you to sit on me but please don't leave rubbish by me'. I'd rather like one of these in my garden.

This stage of the walk takes you to the lovely little settlement of Bathampton, which until 1983 was the site of William Harbutt's plasticine factory. Today, it offers the walker a rather nice spot for a mid-morning break with the George Inn conveniently located right next to the towpath.

After just two miles I'd really begun to get the sense that this was a canal which had really re-engaged people. From walkers to cyclists, holiday cruisers to houseboats there just seemed to be a lot of people making use of this waterway again. I was really intrigued by the idea of living on the canal. Clearly lots of people were and there was an obvious sense of community. So, I arranged to meet the Leake family, one of this growing band of new canal users who've made it their home.

I met Fleur, Johnny and their two boys just outside Bathampton where they invited me to step on board. Their lovely Dutch barge is also their full time home which they simply move up and down the canal, moving in between the different temporary moorings that are available. Fleur explained that six years ago they found the boat and decided to make a new life by living on the water. It seems they haven't looked back since. 'It is so friendly, such a really big feeling of community. We all watch out for each other, watch out for each other's kids, we all share lifts to school. It's a lovely way to live', explained Fleur. I even discovered that Theo, their youngest son was born on board; he quite literally 'popped

ABOVE: The nineteenth century Dundas Aqueduct.

out on the rug'. They'd certainly made their boat so lovely and homely it would have been too easy to linger. But I had to tear myself away from the promise of a nice brew and get back to the walk.

The next port of call is Dundas Wharf, originally built to serve the nearby Conkwell quarries, enabling the distinctive local stone to be transported by boat. This was also an important junction for the canal builders. Here, they faced the problem of crossing the River Avon. For this the Canal Company brought in John Rennie, a rising star of civil engineering and someone who, at the turn of the nineteenth century, was making a name for himself in the world of bridge building.

The aqueduct was completed in 1805 and named after Charles Dundas, the first chairman of the Canal Company.

Rennie might not have achieved the fame of his engineering contemporaries like James Brindley and Thomas Telford but the Dundas Aqueduct is considered to be his crowning achievement, as well as a masterpiece of classical-style architecture. Not only is it a listed structure, but in 1951 it became the first ever canal structure to be designated a 'Scheduled Ancient Monument'. But the fragile nature of the stone led to erosion. The aqueduct developed leaks and by the 1950s was unusable. For a brief period in the 70s you could walk along the dry canal bed of the aqueduct and it's since been relined, restored, reopening for use in 1984.

A heron soaks up the silence of the canal.

From Dundas, you head into the Limpley Stoke Valley. Although this bit of the canal looks as flat as the rest of it, you are actually on a slope here and this is the section of the waterway that needed the heaviest reinforcement to stop it slipping all the way down into the River Avon. Much of that all-important £25 million lottery grant went into reinforcing this stretch.

From here it's only a short walk to John Rennie's next creation, the Avoncliff Aqueduct, which takes the canal across the River Avon for a second time. It's certainly a good-looking structure but, in engineering terms this is perhaps something he might have wanted to keep quiet about. Immediately after its completion in 1801, its central arch sagged and it has had to be repaired many times since. The porous Bath stone was

Colourful boats line the way.

his undoing and Rennie is said to have regretted ever using it.

The next mile was probably the most bustling stretch of towpath I'd been on. It also leads to the halfway point of the walk at Bradford-on-Avon, a kind of mini Bath, where the older buildings are made from the same Jurassic sandstone. Records of trading in this area go back as far as the fourteenth century. As you approach the town you can't help but notice the impressive tithe barn on the left hand side of the towpath, which has one of the largest stone roofs in Europe. It was certainly a sign of things to come and by the mid nineteenth century business on the canal was flourishing. The wharf here was a busy distribution centre where goods were loaded and dispatched by boat for delivery around the world.

STAGE 3

Bradford-on-Avon to Caen Hill Locks

A colourful narrowboat brightens the towpath near Bathampton on the Kennet & Avon Canal.

The Kennet & Avon Canal was profitable for some forty years but the rise of the railway network was to seal its fate. Brunel's railway arrived in 1840 linking London to Bristol in less than three hours. The canal could barely compete. The Great Western Railway Company eventually took over the canal in 1852 hiking tolls to squeeze business out until the canal was hardly used at all.

Although the rail company had a statutory obligation to keep the canal navigable, over the following decades and into the twentieth century it fell into disrepair, and activity on the canal had all but ground to a halt. That was until the summer of 1940, when allied code breakers intercepted a message from Nazi headquarters that placed the nation in jeopardy. Hitler had given his directive to invade Britain and this stretch of the canal played a crucial role in responding to the nation's fear of a possible invasion from the south. The canal was a ready made boundary along which to organise a defensive barrier, known as the GHQ line.

Now, I'd already walked some of this section of the Kennet & Avon Canal around Seend before and I knew that there was something lurking on the other side of the brambles – dotted all along the canal are pillboxes. So, I arranged to meet local historian, Hugh Pihlens, to find out how the canal intriguingly found a new purpose as Britain's potential last line of defence.

In May 1940, France had been overrun in just six weeks and Hitler was standing at the English Channel thinking that it might just now be possible to invade England. It was a huge threat, and Britain's response was to set up a coastal cluster of defences around the sea, but also to have a series of lines of defence along rivers and canals. One of the most important was here on the Kennet & Avon.

There were a total of eighteen thousand defences built between the end of May and September 1940. Today, six thousand remain. As Hugh Pihlens explained, before the pillboxes were built the canal was pretty much unused and some of the lock gates were damaged and not holding water. 'It was a sad scene but it definitely did play its part. They were able to use the canal where there was water to carry materials for these pillboxes and for all the other defences built along the canal. So it flourished a little, again'.

They were going to be manned by local defence volunteers, the volunteers which Churchill famously first called the Home Guard in a speech to the BBC. This was 'Dad's Army', the men who were too frail or too old to join the armed forces. Although these pillboxes never actually saw active service, they are a lasting monument to the Devizes 'Dad's Army', who were ready and willing to play their part.

A swan enjoys some towpath forraging in Bath.

After coming so close to losing everything in the war, the canal became a symbol representing the value people placed on their identity and heritage. In the years to come the passion with which the public became engaged in its restoration was unprecedented.

Julia approaches her final destination.

The final goal of the walk is now the Caen Hill lock flight at Devizes. This flight of sixteen locks raises the canal 235 feet and it's listed as one of the Seven Wonders of British Waterways. This was a list drawn up by Robert Aickman, the founding father of the Inland Waterways Association over fifty years ago. Although it's not the steepest flight in the UK, this was Rennie's solution for negotiating Caen Hill. Each lock is paired with its own reservoir to keep it topped up with water and even these now have a life of their own, with animals and plants making a home here.

After years of campaigning, fundraising and backbreaking volunteer work, when the canal was officially re-opened by the Queen in 1990, the Caen Hill flight of locks was the final icing on the cake. It was the last part to be built when the canal first opened in 1810 and the last part to be restored 180 years later.

For over two centuries this beautiful waterway has rolled on the waves of varying fortunes and continues to do so. The Kennet and Avon Canal is a real story of our time, a true story of survival.

Keep boat
forward of
cill marker

LEFT: Caen Hill Locks, one of the Seven Wonders of British Waterways.
ABOVE: Julia enjoys the views from the top of the Caen Hill flight of locks.

Bath is well served by national rail services. For more information on travelling here and for maps of the city consult Visit Bath:
visitbath.co.uk/site/travel-and-maps
At the end of the walk in Devizes the nearest main line railway stations are at Chippenham, Pewsey, Swindon and Westbury. For more information: www.devizes.org.uk/visiting/getting-here.html
Recommended maps: OS Explorer 155, 156

INDEX

A

Aonach Mor 75
Archers, The 51
Avon Valley 89,
    91
Avoncliff
    Aqueduct
    100

B

Banavie 62, 69,
    71
Bath 85, 87, 89-
    95, 100
Bathampton 90,
    96, 97, 102
Bath Top Lock
    92
Ben Nevis 69,
    72
Birmingham 7,
    39-41, 43-
    45, 47-51,
    53, 58, 59

Bournville 49
Bradford-on-
    Avon 5, 89,
    96, 101, 102
Bristol 40, 86,
    91, 103
Brunel 103

C

Cadbury 48, 49
Caen Hill 87,
    89, 102, 106,
    107, 109
'Canal Mania'
    40, 65, 86
Captain Jones
    26, 27
Castell Dinas
    Bran 20, 21
Cleveland
    House 93-95
Coast-to-Coast
    61
Conkwell
    Quarries 98
Corpach 65-69,
    83

D

Dad's Army
    104
Devizes 89,
    104, 106,
    109
Dundas
    Aqueduct
    98, 99

E

Edgbaston 47
Edward Elgar
    43, 57, 59
'Eirlys' 34
Eisteddfod 28
Ellesmere Canal
    16

F

Fay Weldon 51
Fort William
    61, 65, 69,
    79, 83

G

Gairlcohy 65,
    80, 82
Gas Street
    Basin 41, 44,
    50
GHQ Line 103
'Girl Patricia'
    71
Gloucester 40
Godfrey
    Baseley 51
'Gongoozling'
    32
Great Glen
    61,65, 69,
    76, 79, 81,
    83
Great Western
    Railway
    Company
    103

H

Hawkesley 51
Highland
    Clearances
    62, 70
Hitler 103, 104
Home Guard
    104
Horseshoe Falls
    16, 17, 19,
    20, 22, 23

I

Inverness 65,
    79

J

Jane Austen 95
John Rennie 54,
    98, 100
'Jones the
    Boats' 34,
    36

K

Kennet & Avon
    Canal Trust
    92

L

Limpley Stoke
    Valley 100
Llangollen 5,
    13, 15, 16,
    20, 21, 23,
    25-32, 37

Llangollen Horse-drawn boats 26, 27
Loch Lochy 9, 65, 78, 81, 83
Loch Ness 65
London 17, 86, 91, 103
'Lord of the Glens' 67
Loy Sluices 72, 74, 76, 78, 79

M

Midlands, The 39, 43, 86
Model village 49
Moy Swing Bridge 62, 80

N

Narrow Boat 53
Navvies 71, 79
Nazis 103
Neptune's Staircase 62, 66, 70-73

P

Pavarotti 28
Pentland Firth 67
Pentre Felin 20, 24, 26
Pillboxes 103, 104
Plasticine 97
Pontcysllte Aqueduct 13, 15, 17, 19, 21, 24, 30, 33, 37
Pulteney Bridge 84, 91

R

Richard & George Cadbury 49
River Avon 85, 90, 91, 98, 100
River Dee 15, 17, 21, 23, 25, 32, 36
River Severn 16, 39, 40, 43, 52, 57, 58

S

Scheduled Ancient Monument 80, 99

Scotland 61, 62, 65, 67, 73
Shengain Aqueduct 73, 74
Ship canal 70
Sir Henry Gough-Calthorpe 47
Somerset 91
'Stream through the Skies' 15, 36
Sydney Gardens 94, 95

T

Tardebigge 44, 51, 52-54
Tardebigge Locks 41, 43, 46, 52, 53
Thomas Telford 15, 16, 19, 22, 24, 25, 29, 32, 33, 35, 36, 61, 62, 65, 67-71, 73-76, 79, 81, 82, 99
Tom Rolt 53
Trevor Basin 34

V

Vale of Llangollen 21

W

Wales 16, 19, 21, 25, 28, 36, 68
White Star Line 27
William Harbutt 97
Worcester 5, 39-41, 43, 45, 47, 48, 50-53, 56-59
Worcester Porcelain Museum 57
Worcester Royal Porcelain 43
Word Heritage Site 15, 36, 91
'Workshop of the World' 40

Canal Walks with Julia Bradbury

AV9827 DVD £17.99   Free p&p*

The complete television series, presented by Julia Bradbury, as broadcast on BBC TV, featuring all four episodes.

*postage and packing usually £3.00

Also available on DVD:

AB2001 Blu-ray
£19.99
AV9677 DVD
£14.99
Railway Walks
with Julia Bradbury

AV9620
Wainwright Walks
Series One
£14.99

AV9641
Wainwright Walks
Series Two
£14.99

AV9676
Wainwright Walks
Coast to Coast
£14.99

AV9590
Wainwright Walks
Complete Collection
£49.99

AV9917
Wainwright Walks
Series One and Two
£24.99

Order now from www.acornmediauk.com or telephone
the UK customer orderline on 0845 123 2312.
Don't forget to use promotional code CWFL for free p&p on Canal Walks.